Puppies

Alex Kuskowski

A Division of ABDO

ABDO
Publishing Company

Consulting Editor, Diane Craig, M.A./Reading Specialist

visit us at www.abdopublishing.com

Published by ABDO Publishing Company, a division of ABDO, P.O. Box 398166, Minneapolis, Minnesota 55439. Copyright © 2014 by Abdo Consulting Group, Inc. International copyrights reserved in all countries. No part of this book may be reproduced in any form without written permission from the publisher. SandCastle™ is a trademark and logo of ABDO Publishing Company.

Printed in the United States of America, North Mankato, Minnesota
062013
092013

 PRINTED ON RECYCLED PAPER

Editor: Liz Salzmann
Content Developer: Alex Kuskowski
Cover and Interior Design and Production: Mighty Media, Inc.
Photo Credits: Shutterstock, Thinkstock

Library of Congress Cataloging-in-Publication Data

Kuskowski, Alex.
  Puppies / by Alex Kuskowski ; consulting editor, Diane Craig.
     p. cm. -- (Baby animals)
  Audience: 4-9.
  ISBN 978-1-61783-840-8
1. Puppies--Juvenile literature. I. Craig, Diane. II. Title.
  SE427.K87 2014
  636.7'07--dc23
                    2012049951

SandCastle™ Level: Beginning

SandCastle™ books are created by a team of professional educators, reading specialists, and content developers around five essential components—phonemic awareness, phonics, vocabulary, text comprehension, and fluency—to assist young readers as they develop reading skills and strategies and increase their general knowledge. All books are written, reviewed, and leveled for guided reading, early reading intervention, and Accelerated Reader® programs for use in shared, guided, and independent reading and writing activities to support a balanced approach to literacy instruction. The SandCastle™ series has four levels that correspond to early literacy development. The levels are provided to help teachers and parents select appropriate books for young readers.

| Emerging Readers | Beginning Readers | Transitional Readers | Fluent Readers |
| (no flags) | (1 flag) | (2 flags) | (3 flags) |

Contents

Puppies

A young dog is a puppy.

Puppies are playful.

They are great pets.

Puppies are born in a **litter**. They have brothers and sisters.

Puppies drink milk for their first four weeks. After four weeks, they eat puppy food.

Boomer is taking a nap. Puppies sleep more than 14 hours a day.

Molly walks her puppy every day. Puppies need exercise.

Aidan's puppy, Bella, is whining. Puppies whine, bark, howl, and **growl** to **communicate**.

Casey gnaws on a ball.
Puppies like to chew
on things.

Eli is training his puppy. He **rewards** her with a treat. Puppies learn quickly.

Puppies grow fast. After two years, most puppies are fully grown.

Did You Know?

● ●

▶ Most dogs live between 10 and 14 years.

▶ Dogs come in many different sizes. But all dogs have 321 bones and 42 teeth.

▶ Each puppy's nose has a **unique** print. It's like a human fingerprint.

▶ Puppies cannot hear or see until they are one week old.

Puppy Quiz

Read each sentence below. Then decide whether it is true or false.

1. Puppies are born in a **litter**.

2. Puppies only sleep three hours a day.

3. Molly takes her puppy for a walk once a week.

4. Bella whines to **communicate**.

5. Puppies like to chew on things.

Answers: 1. True 2. False 3. False 4. True 5. True

23

Glossary

communicate – to share ideas, information, or feelings.

growl – to make a deep, low, threatening sound.

litter – a group of baby animals, such as puppies, born at the same time.

reward – to give something to someone for helping out or doing something correctly.

unique – the only one of its kind.